The Ruby Red's Affair

Also by Sandra Renew and published by Ginninderra Press
Projected on the Wall
Who Sleeps at Night
The Orlando Files

Sandra Renew

The Ruby Red's Affair

The Ruby Red's Affair is a work of fiction and imagination.

The Ruby Red's Affair
ISBN 978 1 76109 265 7
Copyright © text Sandra Renew 2022
Cover image: Alberto Bobbera on Unsplash

First published 2022 by
GINNINDERRA PRESS
PO Box 3461 Port Adelaide 5015
www.ginninderrapress.com.au

Contents

Part 1
- Bardo — 11
- Zan and Jo — 12
- Wheel Man — 13
- Jimmy Choo-Shoes — 15

Part 2
- Queen's rules — 19
- Is the queen a bloke? — 20
- cost of trans, she won't go there — 21
- The dilemma of the gender-ambiguous… — 22
- is she herself? — 23
- for a brief time, in the eyes of others, she becomes a man… — 24
- all in love with Clancy — 26
- girls learn attitude — 27

Part 3
- Ruby Red's — 31
- Pick-up with queer — 32
- Outing — 34

Part 4
- Flirt — 37
- On watching Dr Who — 38
- Dancer watched — 39
- all in the name — 40

Part 5
- Deal-breaker — 43
- Deal-breaker: Face the music — 44

Part 6
- it's pretty straightforward: Scoot Valuti's lament — 47

a stake in queer	48
Kaos (T-shirt)	50
Afterwards, and afterword	51

Her name is Scoot Valuti and it is both 1970 and 2021 and all the time between.

Scoot Valuti undertakes a visit to a local lesbian bar/night club, meets up with her friends, and, in search of a lifelong loving relationship based on mutual respect and appreciation, has a brief flirtation which results, sadly, in a serious affair which lasts a nanosecond and ends badly.

She angsts and obsesses about clothes and hair and image. Faced with a smorgasbord of gender possibilities, she chooses…

This is a story of a going out, coming out, strangers as friends, finding THE ONE, finding herself, but not knowing herself, and the Bad End she comes to when she does not manage the expectations of others.

Part 1

Scoot Valuti muses on her general malaise.

Uncertainty is evident in the psyche in her search for THE ONE and we are introduced to her friends.

Bardo

in the low light of the bardo   between death and rebirth
soul is disconnected   my body goes on without me
known to all as one thing   know myself in limbo
coming out leaves me   in liminal uncertainty

waiting for the axe to fall   to be 'outed' publicly
situation flouting   all the rules   of safety and resolution

in the bardo, still in limbo   an unfinished consternation
demanding resolution   of my untenable condition

look around me in the cosmos   making mental notes
of the people who assume   the safety of normality

never making any statement   to clarify their position
that puts me on the outside   with no hesitation

leaves me looking for the public space   where gender is together
the answer and the question.

acknowledgement of limbo   shine some light into the bardo.

Her friends gossip and mooch, drink too much, solve each other's problems and lavishly offer her free advice. She remembers her mother, teachers, everyone, drumming it in: you are known by the friends you keep! And feels a vague frisson of concern. There's Zan and Jo (although obviously they haven't met for coffee for some time, being incarcerated in a foreign nick), the Wheelman and Jimmy Choo-Shoes!

Zan and Jo

Zan and Jo, darlings of their mothers
grow into fairy elf kings in the garden dress-ups
in tinsel crowns and leggings
together they have things sorted

at high school graduation
Zan and Jo come out together
to the dance and then the town

together, fairy kings in Oxford Street and Mardi Gras
until they trip to foreign lands
put cocaine in their handbags
are caught up in the traffic

laws   in public views and in the media
fairy elf kings no longer   step into reality
together they come unsorted

disaster past the making
Zan and Jo no longer   they're
dying in a foreign jail
not their idea of fairyland

And then there's the Wheelman, always a handy ambiguous escort when required for a foray into the night, in the search for THE ONE.

Wheel Man

he started as a wheel man, ended up a tycoon
from driving for the main man
he becomes the main man

and in the world of guns and cons
his secret life, a pretty boy, was open
to interpretation

unpredictable encounters
ya know I ain't queer   me neither
beats and bars, a bagman   a hit man

big money ain't queer   dirty money neither
laundered on an island   beautiful and distant
in the Caribbean

then one night the unthinkable
in a penthouse on the skyline
only once he let his guard down

a street boy   one just started as a wheel man
a pretty boy in deep disguise
is shown to be a girl

so then we have the wheel man   lifetime as a con man
gender open   to interpretation
reveals   that   all along

recognition of his toughness   looked on falsely as a man –
a David Bowie kind of beauty, true
but underneath it all he's a woman and a lesbian

you know she ain't queer   she's not neither   she's the Wheelman
and Jimmy Choo-Shoes, who are they? A friend in shoes, indeed…

Jimmy Choo-Shoes

he chose, as appropriate, Jimmy Choo Romy 100 shoes at
$668.00 AU with the delicate rise of the sole to an extremely
serious heel

he shopped for them on Amazon, free standard delivery
not Gumtree or
Lifeline's Op Shop, donated and pre-loved

their appearance in the line-up, second row of singers,
is most notable
among the standard black of old boots, best shoes, gym
shoes, trodden-down court shoes, workday lace-ups, other
well-used slip-ons –

my gaze follows from gorgeous shoe to trousered leg to
ironed shirt, hair wet-combed and slicked back above his ears

when the bodies move
he places his feet just so, patent leather pumps,
just shoes, but gorgeous shoes

Part 2

What's a girl to wear?

Do you think that clothes make the man, the girl, the woman, the queen? Do you think that what you wear is a small thing? The stories we tell say different, say life and death.

This part of the story is where Scoot Valuti has an encounter with a drag queen in the car park at a local lesbian bar, causing her to question the whole existential nature of gender presentation and how this can cause confusion and general mayhem in the Universe.

Queen's rules

when the queen gives her the finger
in the dangerous murk of the multistorey car park
she hesitates
can she take her on, take her out?
her Doris Day hair, Diana Ross dress
eyes made up to kill and talons green with glitter

she decides not
backs up
enough to show backing-down intent
allows the black Jeep rumble space through to the exit boom

Just so you know, this is not hypothetical musing, not idle conjecture. Queerness can require disowning, abandoning the country you were born in, for survival, begging at the borders of others for space and a place where your country will not kill you. (Quote from the Wheelman)

Is the queen a bloke?

Carlotta

shot flaming forth   ablaze
flush'd far side of calm

cool

wheel wild   fiery run   six shooters

grappled
man to man
blazed
shaved
reckless

where now   trouble
my share of wine

undone
misspent

live the same life over
never fence my bed

This is an erasure poem from 'The sick stockrider' by Adam Lindsay Gordon (Geoffrey Lehmann and Robert Gray, eds, *Australian Poetry Since 1788*, UNSW Press, 2011, p. 36). Carlotta, who performed at Les Girls until 1992, was one of the first people to have a sex-change operation in Australia. Her story is referenced in a brass plaque set into the footpath in Kings Cross, Sydney, outside the Empire Hotel.

cost of trans, she won't go there

body reconstruction
social preference of the binary
our happiness for the remedy
even with medicare economy
is measured in suicide rate reduction

The dilemma of the gender-ambiguous. Toilet, bathroom, latrine, either way, it's one or the other and you have to run the gauntlet, make a public choice, get there...

in the time before she becomes him
she learns to walk again, to take up more space
fine-tune her hand movements, stop the finger flutter
she knew from early on girly times
use a frown and stop smiling
learns to give her legs room when she sits down

the blouses in the ironing basket change to button-down shirts
slacks with a back zipper now trousers with pleated waist
twin sets give way to v-neck pullovers
bras disappear,
boxer shorts, black nylon socks and white singlets
hang discreetly on the veranda lines

in the time before she becomes him
men's on the left
women's on the right
and either way,
past the laundry well and the public taps
the long, exposed walk
jeers and jibes,
taunts trigger the running away...

is she herself?

In whose eyes, when and where, is she herself? Shapeshifter, witch, shaman, magician. They said you can be anything you want to be. Did they also mean anyone you want to be?

Shaken after her thought-provoking encounter with the driver of the black Jeep, she has second and third thoughts about identity and the existential question raised by the drag queen's challenge…

for a brief time, in the eyes of others, she becomes a man…

they make her a man, the commentators
there's an irony in it
when she's a hero, she looks like a man
when the heat dies from the moment
she is retrieved as a woman
who is they? the commentators, how do they mix this alchemy?
the *déjà la*, the oppressive weight of the always already there

This is an ekphrastic response to 'A mixed-up affair all round' by Frank Moorhouse, commenting on 'The drover's wife' by Henry Lawson (in Frank Moorhouse, ed., *The Drover's Wife: A celebration of a great Australian love affair*, Knopf, 2017, p. 25).

Confusion is all, and it's all in here, and not at all clear who is who and why that might be important.
At what point is it a crime? What is the point of punishment? The old white men and the young, new generation, multicultural, shades of blue and brown men, use their bodies for their anger, believe their bodies are the image, the image is the fuck, the fuck is the power.

all in love with Clancy

they were all in love with Clancy
the old white men (although they were young then)
with pens in their hands
all in thrall to the lean, brown
drover, lord of the horse and moving stock

they wrote him up, built him up
made him more than they could ever be
hero-worship, golden god,
trod over, trod down the words of those
who loved the country not a man

and the crowd went wild for decades,
adulation, immortalising, ANZAC accolades
the old poets, still, see themselves as Clancy

they were all in love with Clancy
with themselves and their words
they knew themselves as Clancy

Not wanting to give any more airtime to the old white male rule makers of the patriarchy, she takes a deep breath and breathes in the new world. 'Get over them. Do your girl thing but give us the hit of your bad dyke attitude.' (Quote from Jimmy Choo-Shoes)

girls learn attitude

girls learn attitude with eye-rolling at the same time we pick
up shoulder-shrugging, the adolescent slouch and whatever –
disguise our dark selves, our naiveté and angel-eyes

girls learn eye-rolling and gut recoil when older men
sing Baby Baby it's only the beginning, the boar-taint
ugliness of men who act like pigs, I know you want it, put
out for me, Baby Baby, eye rolling, shoulder
shrugging whatever…

girls learn the #MeToo movement tweet Twitter (what took you
so long?) an eye roll, a shoulder shrug, until it's not enough
the solution to boar taint is castration…

Boar taint is an offensive odour or taste in pork products made from
uncastrated adult male pigs.

Part 3

The pick-up.

Tonight's the night! In a low-key, desperate kind of way. She's going out. Out into the wild. On the town. Looking for some action, but not really. She's too vanilla, too much looking for long-term, love of my life, soulmate 4EVA, THE ONE.

She's looking into her metaphysics, the meta data of the existential question, summarised as WTF! Who am I? Who am I, really?

When she walks into the bar, this particular, soon-to-be-iconic bar, she feels she has come home, to someone's home at least.

Ruby Red's

Ruby Red's in nineteen-seventy
was fairly dykey
girls only
on Crown Street, Sydney

cruise it
check it out
'who's around? who's up for it?'

Ruby Red's was pretty tender
lots of girls
pretty dykey
for anyone
any pretender

She's at the bar for a reason, and the reason is all around her,
if she has the nerve.

Pick-up with queer

In weeks of coffee-klatch analysis
in café after café, Jimmy Choo-Shoes and the Wheelman

with foresight and hindsight tender   impressed on her
the dangers of all-eggs-in-one-basket hopefulness

and misguided anticipation   this
forensic, latté-fuelled investigation   proves

that everything is temporary
remember everything is possible but everything is temporary
fast stars

fill public space with queer
riff and sizzle   frissons of uncertainty

strange-eyed women show their teeth
smiles provoking invitations   ambiguously

lined up on barstools contiguous
with hooking up   though it's all beneath

public radar   it's at her instigation
and done with alcohol bravado, nervous anticipation

The story's in the image, who is dressed as who; could be the frock, who wears the pants, who does not.

Sitting at the bar, in Ruby Red's she takes her own risks, but she must choose wisely to survive the night, alert to who is being who, being Who.

And, of course, her intention, fuelled by the Wheelman and Jimmy Choo-Shoes, is to Come Out, at least to herself, even if she's not sure of herself.

Outing

it's an outing
a shirt-tucked-in event
white shirt, Dunlop Volleys, so it's formal then

finger pointing,
father's serial disappointment
with a never-in-a-million Girl in a Million
mother murmuring
whatever did we do to you?

Facebook still a misogynist boy dream
not even Twittersphere for twenty years
but word of mouth
and it's out

Part 4

Two minutes to midnight

Is this THE ONE? Now she's Out. She's on the floor. On the scene. In the action. And it's two minutes to midnight.

Flirt

that night in autumn when   in the heat of the shower spray
steam first reappears
that indicates a cooling of the ambient air
a presence unexpected

first signs appear   invisible made visible by flirt
the time is right
air shadowed by the stink of old beer
and fags   smoke and uncertainty

no sign of skirts for this flirt   from hands in pockets
hands everywhere
hover over   settle on   make dampness from their fingerprints
ambiguity of water in air

first flirt alert   that there is more to encounter than first appears
suggests appearances deceive
no skirts   but shirts pants hands in pockets
perhaps she's not

Extrapolating intimacy, we learn from pubs and parties
a plethora of possibilities.

She is the watcher and the watched, the world is observed.
She's a pirate dancer and so is she. They dance the same
dance in the same body, her steps are her steps.
In time and space, you can see both dancer and music,
woman and woman and neither, simultaneously and
interchangeably.

On watching Dr Who

If I die, click here. Is she an alien?
I love her coat. She's saving us from ourselves
her mission statement sorting out fair play throughout the
Universe.

Dancer watched

You think she's dancing for you, and you've picked the music.
You think you're getting what you paid for.
But she's a pirate dancer. She's colonised the space, made the steps her own, demands a ransom for your attentions.
When she flaunts her steps in your face, look away.
She's a pirate dancer. The body and the music are her body and her music.
The steps are her steps, she owns the space, she takes no prisoners.
There is no escape for you.
You do not want your thoughts to be hostage
to the dance she dances, the steps she takes.

She has known the Dancer for 5 minutes. But she can't help thinking… The default circuit is marriage, wedding, THE ONE (the other) – the small plastic replica of bride and groom on top of the cake takes the cake!
And Jimmy Choo-Shoes and the Wheelman know this Dancer – 'she's not for you' they say, shouting over the music and noise and breaking glasses. 'She's too much! Don't let her be your obsession. Don't get your hopes up. Keep your heart in your T-shirt.'

all in the name

it's a loser game where she's not dyke enough
to claim the name

if you don't have the scars and pain
then you you're not allowed to play the game

whose fish? whose bicycle?

there's the butch dyke, femme dyke
in pairs but not-yet-married dykes
vanilla dyke diesel dyke   and   like
discreet dykes

Friends of Dorothy euphemisms
aunties, flannels, in a lesbian way, a lemon,

baby butches, bent dykes and bike dykes
so campy for the cruise game

can't bridge the apprehension, tension
like Stonewall and Mardi Gras
political intervention

Part 5

Deal-breaker

Above the roar and sweat and boom, under the epilepsy-inducing strobe lights, flicker-vertigo amid the unrestrained glitter and eye make-up, the Dancer is revealed as a Philistine…ridicules the 'lowbrowness' of country music, no flicker of recognition for Dolly Parton, Emmylou Harris, never heard of Buffy Sainte-Marie, the protest music of Joan Baez. ABBA is the politically incorrect representation of the seventies. Really? No shit?

A bottom line is the thud on wooden boards of one hundred Cuban heels in a line dance classic. The Dancer looks askance…wouldn't be seen dead etc…

Truth telling of the Dancer's shortcomings makes her cry. She doesn't know whose deal, but this is a broken deal.

Admittedly, it's a first-world problem, but her dreams and hopes are gone like the night-time scream of a railroad whistle on a long-distance train disappearing over the flatlands.

The Wheelman and Jimmy Choo-Shoes rally in support. If she had long hair they would hold it out of the way as her headache vomits into the stench of the nightclub toilet bowl.

Her disillusion is complete.

Deal-breaker: Face the music

for all the things it could have been
apocalyptic, scary dreams
look ahead a life envision
back-beat beat-up in unison
it was music did us in

music is not binary
insert a truth, fabricate me
into your hypocrisy
what do I owe you who are afraid of me?
won't grieve my life for Eurovision?

compromise in music world
it was music did us in

Part 6

It all ends badly OR the status quo of chaos is maintained

she measures the distance between whatever she is and what she wants –
and who she wants and being who she can be…

she her hers her
she loves her she loves her
weddings are messy
gender oils the discourse
can't move without knowing

it's pretty straightforward: Scoot Valuti's lament

I used to be a lesbian but now my people are the whole alphabet
LGBTIQAAA

drag queens, queenie girls, transgender
effeminate men, butch lesbians
male prostitutes and homeless youth
Auschwitz survivors with arm tattoos and the pink triangle
strangers, queers, what's their angle?

once I was just a lesbian, a dyke, not straight, cis or het

She goes for a performance option,
a deliberate confusion transfusion, gender negotiation,
what you see is maybe not what you get...
Should she dress the part? A trousers and waistcoat option?
Befuddle forensics, she wants to continue as an analytic
viewing fiction.

a stake in queer

in Shakespeare's plays, most days, a boy in a dress was required
– a boy to be a girl, being a girl. and it was normal and not
confusing for the audience for Portia, in *The Merchant of
Venice*, a boy being a girl, cross-dressing, disguising himself
being herself being a boy as a persuasive buyer

in 1660, break a leg they said, breaking tradition, Ann
Marshall plays Desdemona in *Othello*, a girl playing a girl.
there was a great to-do, a turnaround for the books, when
Sarah Bernhardt played Hamlet in 1899.
a postcard was made of it, breeches roles being new to the
neural pathways of the possible

she has a stake in queer

for her, these days – most days – it is normal and not confusing
to think of breeches roles
to perform the turnaround
being persuasive being herself being a boy

it's a causeway she has cause to tread
setting down a neural pathway
suit and tie, hair slicked back
her brain not called a nervous system for nothing

'The woman plays to day; mistake me not / No Man in Gown, or Page in Petty-Coat' declaimed Thomas Jordan in 1660 in 'A Prologue to introduce the first Woman that came to act on the Stage, in the Tragedy called the Moor of Venice' (quoted in Vanessa Thorpe, 'Secret lives of women who broke taboo to act in Shakespeare', *Guardian*, 10 April 2016).

After all that, her single-handed overthrowing of the order of the Universe, the smashing of the gender binary, using the women's toilet without being mistaken for a man...after all that, can she settle for a T-shirt, black...no need for a frock, over the top...
Can she settle for a basic non-threatening, but always challenging, nomenclature, lesbian, feminist, dyke, an identity of calm chaos?

She lives as chaos
here she is, there he goes.
She is Orlando and so is he, a disruption of the Universe,
the social order stands in disarray
breaking down the gender binary

Virginia Woolf, *Orlando: A biography*, The Hogarth Press, 1928.

Kaos (T-shirt)

Chaos was the first created
Gaia and Erebus   the stabilisers   came later
mayhem and bedlam   world disarray was first the norm of
things

but poetry black is the new dark order   where order is brave
but futile

our bodies are our history and our geography   both
and how we array the body and clothe the limbs and flesh is
central to the disorder
in the social order

so sensitive to small changes
that change from blouse to T-shirt   causes   havoc
calls for water cannon to force back the surge of chaos
wrought by Kaos

Kaos means T-shirt in Bahasa Indonesia.

Afterwards, and afterword

A range of first-world problems, population overload, can we
feed the planet?
environment past its use-by date, asylum seekers, immigration
population mass migration—
What difference does it make?

Enemies of the State, the journalists, lost freedom of the press,
two minutes to midnight urgency, our gods unsettled within us
seeing things from the inside, sliding to the terminus –

In the days we call today's world, dystopia of failed Utopias
looking into our myopia, what we see is romance
drama, more often than usual, starting with a woman
murdered

when we look to family, patriarchy, misogyny
to find the woman's identity, all they say is it's a mystery
not a conundrum laced with urgency
she's a dyke

we have mythological connectivity, Google is our urban god
unrepentant our families fail to teach us, cannot show us
will not unlock
the myths
of growing up a dyke

showing us now our real gods, wild women, idolise our heroes,
Audre Lorde, Judith Butler, Julia Kristeva, Hélène Cixous
family line is not my bloodline
blood can be the lifeline that kills us in our lifetime
outrageous hypocrisy sucks all meaning from diversity

charging all of the community to vote on me
my value as citizen where I'm one step from the hunters
one step from the bullies   kindergarten to corporation
threatening my safety

looking for two keys turned together
releasing straight relationships
from a straitjacketed conservative
to something more ambivalent

for survival I learn attitude, a finger,
don't fuck with me, my byline
quipping *you're a sorry human being
with no redeeming quality*

the world of my ancestors places me
in genealogy
without looking for a byline or family tree

www.ingramcontent.com/pod-product-compliance
Lightning Source LLC
Chambersburg PA
CBHW062205100526
44589CB00014B/1954